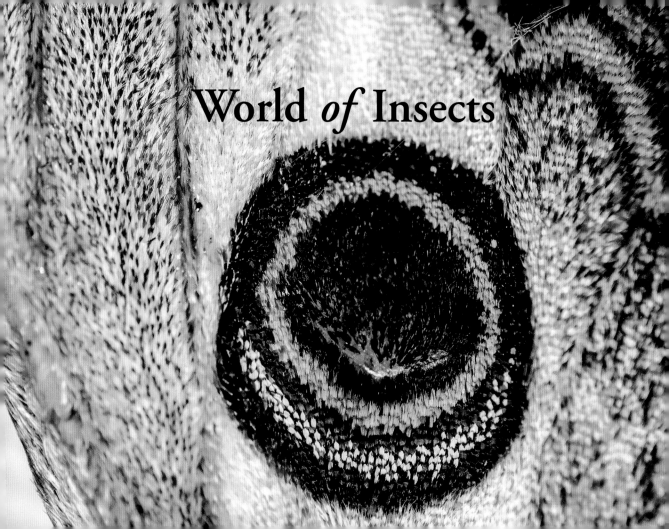

World *of* Insects

World of

Insects

CONTENTS

Introducing the World of Insects

With new species being discovered and identified on a daily basis nobody is quite sure exactly how many species of insects can currently be found on Earth. One thing for sure is that it is in excess of one million. They occupy every imaginable niche, from pollinators through to waste disposal, and their survival and ability to flourish is essential for our ecosystems to function efficiently. In short, without insects we are all doomed.

However, our insect populations are under threat like never before, from habitat destruction, global warming and artificial insecticides which are affecting bug populations on a grand scale. With a mass extinction being mooted many species will be lost before we even realise that they exist.

The various insect forms and societies are quite remarkable. They have seemingly evolved to fill every niche. There are outrageous-looking giraffe weevils with long necks, giant beetles that look too big to fly, and hoppers and butterflies so bright as to be almost unbelievable. Some of the macro shots in this book reveal forms that would look at home in an alien sci-fi movie. And of course there are complex societies in families such as ants, bees and termites.

There are incredible lifecycles too, including the oft-quoted egg-caterpillar-chrysalis-butterfly cycle which is more or less replicated in many other insect orders, while other insects see progression through the development of a series on nymphs which look like miniature versions of the adults.

For the purposes of classification, this book draws on *Insects of the World* by Paul Zborowski (Reed New Holland).

From the common to the rare, *World of Insects* distils the extraordinary diversity of the insect world down into about 250 images illustrating nearly 250 species and as wide a variety of the different insect forms as possible from 24 orders. We hope that you enjoy this book and its amazing images, and that it contributes towards inspiring further interest in insects and their conservation worldwide.

Bristletail species

EUROPE

Long-tailed Silverfish *Ctenolepisma longicaudata*
NORTHERN HEMISPHERE

MAYFLIES – EPHEMEROPTERA

Mayfly larva *Ecdyonurus* species
EUROPE

Mayfly adult

EUROPE

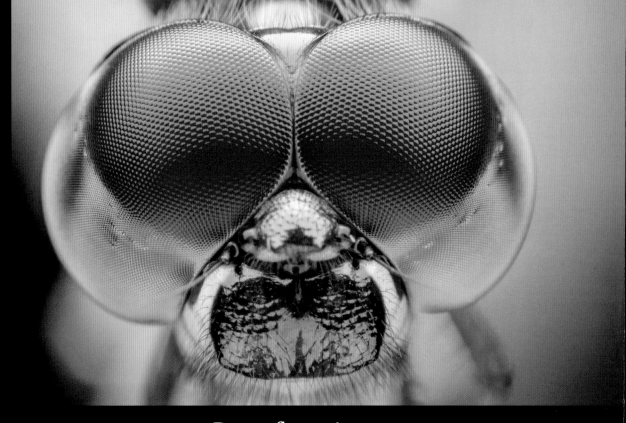

Dragonfly species

ASIA

Dragonfly species
ASIA

Green-eyed Hawker *Aeshna isoceles*

EUROPE AND NORTH AFRICA

Twelve-spotted Skimmer *Libellula pulchella*
NORTH AMERICA

Scarlet Percher *Diplacodes haematodes*
AUSTRALIA AND NEW GUINEA

Broad-bodied Chaser *Libellula depressa*
EURASIA

Emperor Dragonfly *Anax imperator* – larva
AFRICA AND EURASIA

Green Darner *Anax junius*

NORTH AMERICA

Australian Emperor *Anax papuensis*
NEW GUINEA, AUSTRALIA AND NEW ZEALAND

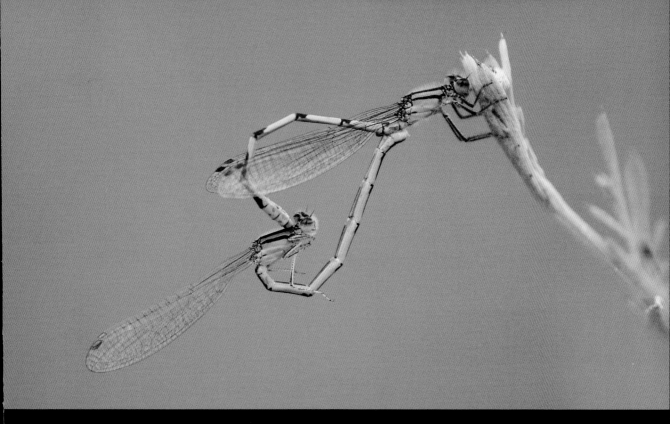

Azure Damselfly *Coenagrion puella*

EURASIA

Small Red-eyed Damselfly *Erythromma viridulum*

Beautiful Demoiselle *Calopteryx virgo*
EURASIA AND NORTH AFRICA

Eastern Red Damsel *Amphiagrion saucium*
NORTH AMERICA

Damselfly larva

Stonefly larva
NORTH AMERICA

Stonefly adult
ASIA

Forest cockroach

ASIA

Hissing cockroach *Princisia vanwaerebeki*

MADAGASCAR

Cave cockroach
CENTRAL AMERICA

Giant Burrowing Cockroach *Macropanesthia rhinoceros*
AUSTRALIA

German Cockroach *Blattella germanica*
WORLDWIDE

Termite soldier

ASIA

Termite species

ASIA

Yellow-necked Dry-wood Termite *Kalotermes flavicollis*
EUROPE

Termite mound

AFRICA

Termite species

ASIA

Termite mounds

AUSTRALIA

European Mantis *Mantis religiosa*

Mantis species

Flower mantis

ASIA

Spiny Flower Mantis *Pseudocreobotra wahlbergii*

Bark mantis
ASIA

Bark mantis *Gonypeta brigittae*

ASIA

Orchid mantis *Hymenopus coronatus*

ASIA

European Earwig *Forficula auricularia*
NORTHERN HEMISPHERE

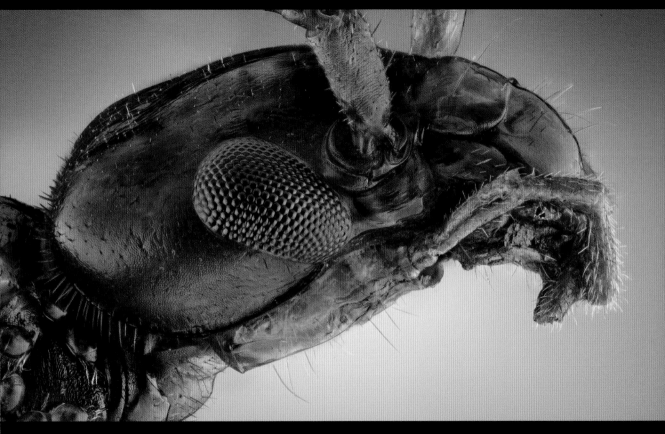

European Earwig *Forficula auricularia*
NORTHERN HEMISPHERE

Earwig species

Earwig species

ASIA

Earwig species

Two-spotted Cricket *Gryllus bimaculatus*
EURASIA AND AFRICA

Striped rainforest cricket
AUSTRALIA

Cricket species

ASIA

Cricket species

ASIA

European Mole Cricket *Gryllotalpa gryllotalpa*
EUROPE

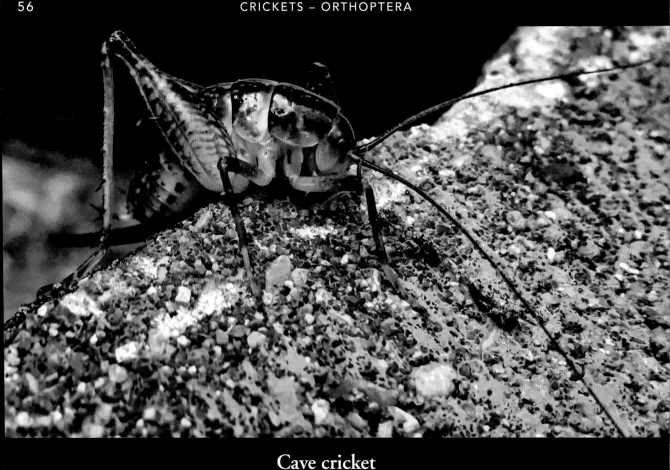

Cave cricket

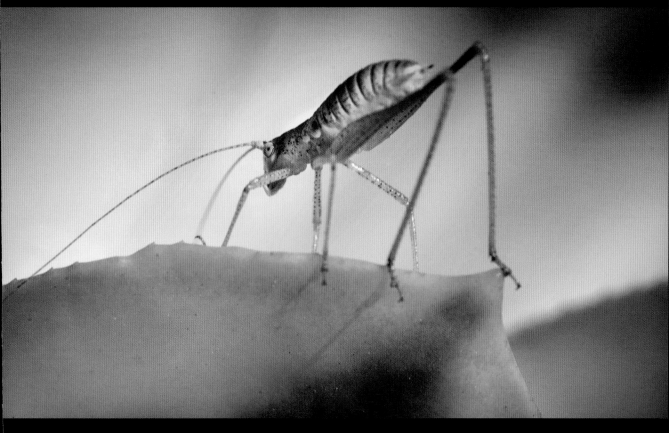

Bush cricket nymph

NORTH AMERICA

Rainforest bush cricket
SOUTH AMERICA

Bush cricket *Bradyporus dasypus*
EURASIA

Bush cricket *Saga pedo*
EURASIA

Green Tree Cricket *Truljalia hibinonis*
JAPAN

Katydid

ASIA

Katydid *Eulophophyllum lobulatum*
BORNEO

Short-winged Conehead   *Conocephalus dorsalis*
EURASIA

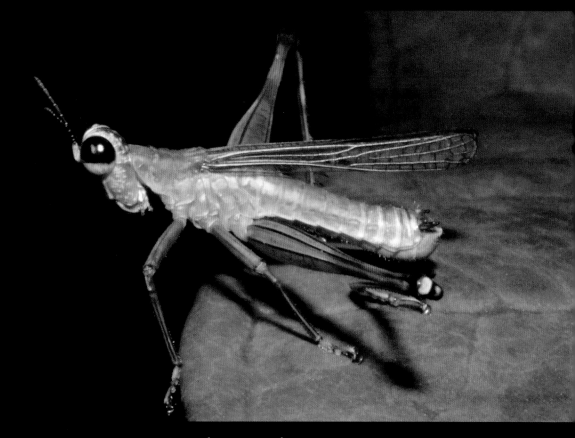

Monkey grasshopper
CENTRAL AMERICA

Katydid or conehead *Neoconocephalus* species
ASIA

Lesser Marsh Grasshopper *Chorthippus albomarginatus*
EURASIA

Stone Grasshopper *Ocnerodes fallaciosus*
EURASIA

Painted Grasshopper *Dactylotum bicolor*

NORTH AMERICA AND MEXICO

Gold Grasshopper *Chrysochraon dispar*
EURASIA

Desert Locust *Schistocerca gregaria*
ASIA AND AFRICA

Desert Locust *Schistocerca gregaria*

ASIA AND AFRICA

Grasshopper species

AFRICA

New Zealand Stick Insect *Clitarchus hookeri*
NEW ZEALAND

Stick insect
ASIA

Giant Prickly Stick Insect *Extatosoma tiaratum*

Green leaf insect
ASIA

Spiny leaf insect

ASIA

Barkfly

EUROPE

Booklice

WORLDWIDE

Body Louse *Pediculus humanus humanus*
WORLDWIDE

Head Louse *Pediculus humanus capitus*
WORLDWIDE

Stink bug

EURASIA

Southern Green Stink Bug *Nezara viridula*
EUROPE

Minstrel Bug *Graphosoma lineatum*
EUROPE

Green shield bug

ASIA

Hibiscus Harlequin Bug *Tectocoris diophthalmus*
AUSTRALIA AND NEW GUINEA

Western Conifer Seed Bug *Leptoglossus occidentalis*
EUROPE

Common Backswimmer *Notonecta glauca*
EURASIA

Lesser Water Boatman *Corixa punctata*
EURASIA

Common Pond Skater *Gerris lacustris*

EURASIA

Assassin bug nymph
ASIA

Assassin bug

AUSTRALIA

Dock Bug *Coreus marginatus*
EURASIA

Mirid bug (with ant)
ASIA

Cicada *Salvazana mirabilis*

ASIA

Silver-bellied Cicada *Tibicen pruinosa*
NORTH AMERICA

Walker's Cicada *Meimuna opalifera* – hatching

ASIA

17-year periodical cicada
NORTH AMERICA

Planthopper
NORTH AMERICA

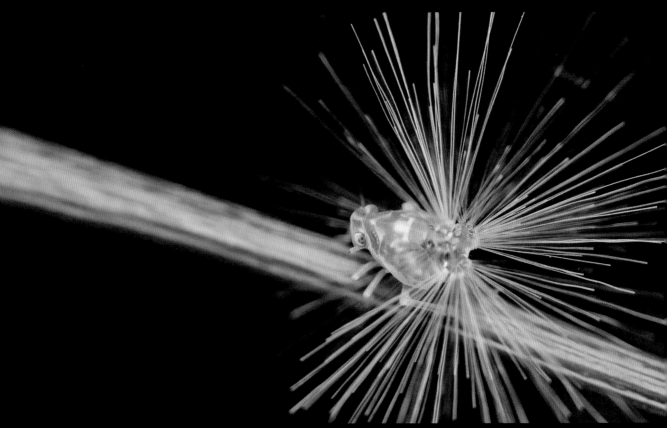

Planthopper
ASIA

Treehopper

ASIA

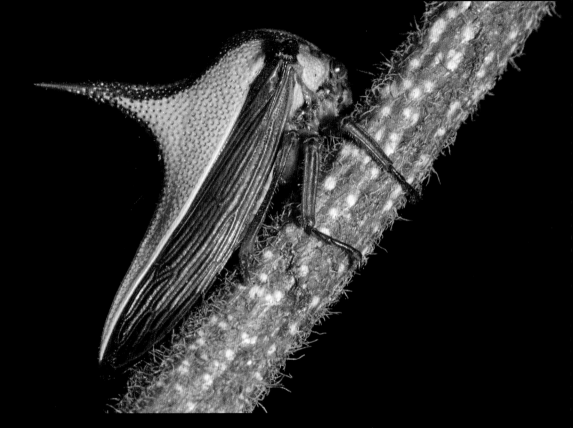

Thorn Treehopper *Umbonia crassicornis*
CENTRAL AMERICA

Lanternfly

ASIA

White-winged Lanternfly *Pyrops astarte*

ASIA

Froghopper larva
JAPAN

Leafhopper *Bothrogonia* species
ASIA

Treehopper
ASIA

Aphid species

EURASIA

Eucalyptus Psylla *Glycaspis brimblecombei*

Cotton Mealybug *Phenacoccus solenopsis*

WORLDWIDE

THRIPS – THYSANOPTERA

Onion Thrips *Thrips tabaci*
WORLDWIDE

Thrips species

EURASIA

Alderfly *Sialis* species
EUROPE

Alderfly larva
EUROPE

Dobsonfly adult

NORTH AMERICA

Dobsonfly adult

ASIA

Dobsonfly adult
ASIA

Dobsonfly larva – also known as a hellgrammite

NORTH AMERICA

Spotted Snakefly *Phaeostigma notata*
EURASIA

Snakefly larva

EURASIA

Lacewing eggs

ASIA

Larva of Common Green Lacewing *Chrysoperla carnea*
EURASIA AND NORTH AFRICA

Lacewing adult

ASIA

Lacewing adult

EURASIA

Owlfly

EURASIA

Owlfly

ASIA

Antlion larva

EURASIA

Antlion larva pit for trapping prey
ASIA

Antlion adult

ASIA

Antlion adult

EURASIA

Spoonwing *Nemoptera coa*
EURASIA

Mantisfly adult
ASIA

Blue Ground Beetle   *Carabus intricatus*

EURASIA

Golden Ground Beetle *Carabus auratus*

Tiger beetle

ASIA

Tiger beetle
ASIA

Tiger beetle

EURASIA

Bombardier beetle
ASIA

Great Diving Beetle *Dytiscus marginalis*
EURASIA

Diving beetle *Dytiscus* **species – larva feeding on a tadpole**
NORTH AMERICA

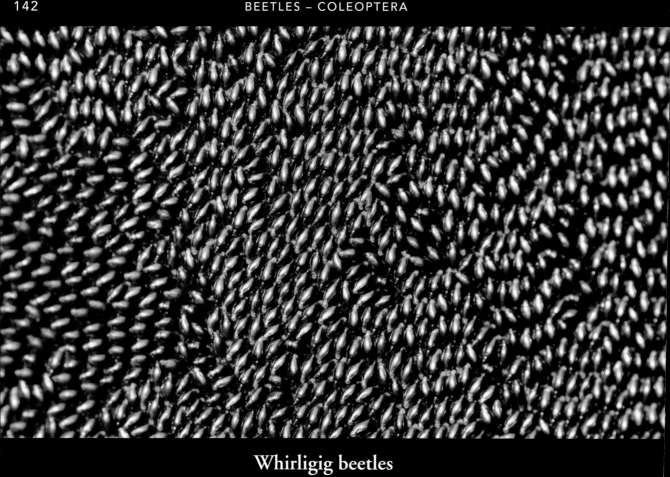

Whirligig beetles
NORTH AMERICA

Burying beetle *Nicrophorus orbicollis*
NORTH AMERICA

Rove beetle *Emus hirtus*

EUROPE

Devil's Coach-horse *Ocypus olens*
EURASIA

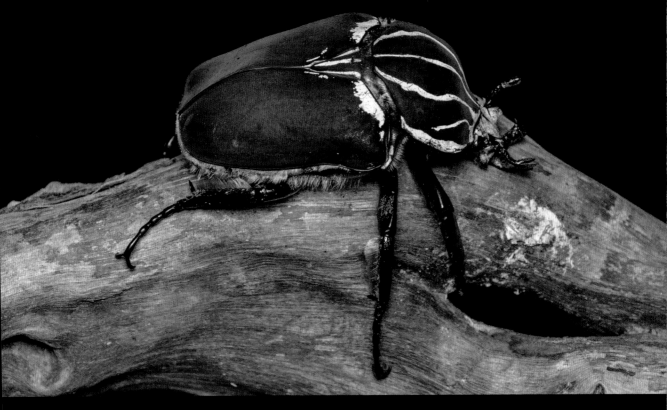

Goliath beetle *Goliathus goliatus*
AFRICA

Polyphemus Beetle *Mecynorrhina polyphemus*

Rose Chafer *Cetonia aurata*

EURASIA

Garden Chafer *Phyllopertha horticola*
EURASIA

Cockchafer *Melolontha melolontha*
EURASIA

Flower chafer

EURASIA

Fiddler Beetle *Eupoecilia australasiae*
AUSTRALIA

Hercules Beetle *Dynastes hercules*
SOUTH AMERICA

Rhinoceros beetle

ASIA

Rhinoceros beetle
ASIA

Atlas Beetle *Chalcosoma atlas*

ASIA

Dung beetle

AFRICA

Dung beetle

EUROPE

Dung beetle
AFRICA

Stag beetles *Lucanus cervus*
EURASIA

Rainbow Stag Beetle *Phalacrognathus muelleri*

ASIA

Stag beetle
ASIA

Rainbow Jewel Beetle *Chrysochroa fulgens*
ASIA

Banded Jewel Beetle *Chrysochroa buqueti rugicollis*

Seven-spot Ladybird *Coccinella septempunctata*
WORLDWIDE

Harlequin Ladybird *Harmonia axyridis*
WORLDWIDE

Firefly
ASIA

Click beetle

EUROPE

Fungus beetle

ASIA

Oil beetle
NORTH AMERICA

Darkling beetle
ASIA

Thick-legged Flower Beetle *Oedemera nobilis*
EUROPE

Tortoise beetle

ASIA

Longicorn beetle *Batocera rufomaculata*
ASIA

Rosalia Longicorn *Rosalia alpina*

EUROPE

Mango Weevil *Sternochetus mangiferae*
WORLDWIDE

Giraffe Weevil *Trachelophorus giraffa*
MADAGASCAR

Rice Weevil *Sitophilus oryzae*

WORLDWIDE

Brentid beetle *Amorphocephala coronata*

Parasitic male *Stylops* emerging from inside bee

EUROPE

Common Scorpionfly *Panorpa communis*

Scorpionfly

ASIA

Cat Flea *Ctenocephalides felis*
WORLDWIDE

Flea species

Yellow Fever Mosquito *Aedes aegypti*

WORLDWIDE

Mosquito *Culex* species

Cranefly *Tanyptera atrata*
EURASIA

Moth fly *Clogmia albipunctata*
WORLDWIDE

Horsefly *Tabanus* **species**

Twin-lobed Deerfly *Chrysops relictus*
EUROPE

Marsh Snipefly *Rhagio tringarius*

EUROPE

Soldierfly species
AUSTRALIA

Robberfly with prey

ASIA

Stiletto fly *Acrosathe annulata*
EUROPE

Bee fly adult
ASIA

Long-legged fly

ASIA

Marmalade Hoverfly *Episyrphus balteatus*
EURASIA AND NORTH AFRICA

Hornet-mimic hoverfly

EUROPE

Thick-headed fly
ASIA

Fruit fly *Drosophila melanogaster*
WORLDWIDE

Stalk-eyed fly

ASIA

Greenbottle fly
ASIA

Caddisfly adult
EUROPE

Caddisfly larva

Ghost Swift *Hepialus humuli*
EUROPE

Fairy moth
EUROPE

Bagworm moth caterpillar
EUROPE

Sphinx moth
SOUTH AMERICA

Large Red-belted Clearwing *Synanthedon culiciformis*
EUROPE

Feather moth
EUROPE

Burnet moth *Zygaena fausta*
EUROPE

Snout moth *Sacada* species

ASIA

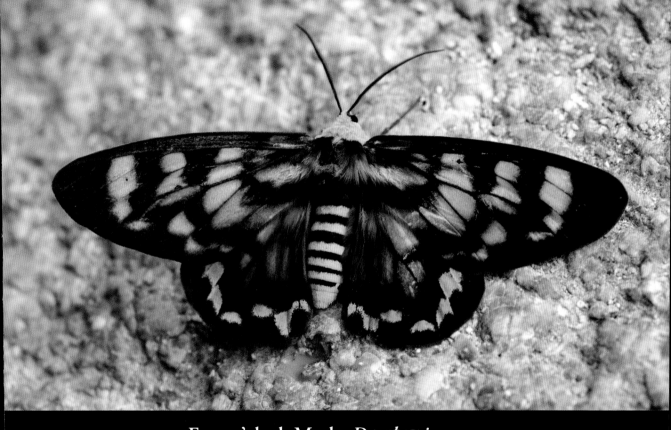

Four o'clock Moth *Dysphania numana*
AUSTRALIA TO INDONESIA

Geometrid moth *Protuliocnemis biplagiata*

ASIA

Hercules Moth *Coscinocera hercules*

Spurge Hawk-moth caterpillar *Hyles euphorbiae*
EURASIA

White-lined Sphinx *Hyles lineata*
NORTH AMERICA

Tussock moth *Euproctis* species
EURASIA

Scarlet Tiger *Callimorpha dominula*
EURASIA

Common Checkered Skipper *Pyrgus communis*

Monarch *Danaus plexippus*

WORLDWIDE

Glasswing species *Greta oto*

SOUTH AMERICA

Red Admiral *Vanessa atalanta*

NORTHERN HEMISPHERE

Leaf butterfly

ASIA

Common Jezebel *Delias eucharis*

AUSTRALIA

Adonis Blue *Lysandra bellargus*

EURASIA

Citrus Swallowtail *Papilio demodocus*
AFRICA

Cairns Birdwing *Ornithoptera euphorion*
AUSTRALIA

Menelaus Blue Morpho *Morpho menelaus*

CENTRAL AMERICA AND SOUTH AMERICA

SAWFLIES – HYMENOPTERA

Gooseberry Sawfly *Nematus ribesii* – larvae

EURASIA

Spitfire Sawfly *Perga affinis* – larvae
AUSTRALIA

Large Rose Sawfly *Arge pagano*
EURASIA

Chalcid wasp
EUROPE

Braconid wasp
SOUTH AMERICA

Braconid wasp

EURASIA

Jewel wasp

ASIA

Velvet ant

Potter wasp

ASIA

Paper wasp *Polistes nimpha*
EURASIA

European Hornet *Vespa crabro*
EURASIA

Beewolf *Philanthus triangulum* – carrying bee prey
EURASIA

Red Wood Ant *Formica rufa*
EURASIA

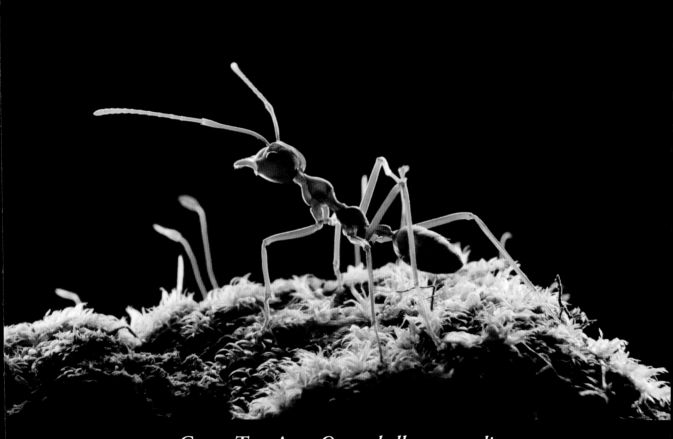

Green Tree Ant *Oecoephylla smaragdina*
ASIA AND AUSTRALIA

Army ant
ASIA

Bullet ant
SOUTH AMERICA

Tropical Carpenter Bee *Xylocopa latipes*
ASIA

White-tailed Bumblebee *Bombus lucorum*

EURASIA

Honey Bee *Apis mellifera*
WORLDWIDE

Blue-banded Bee *Amegilla cingulata*
AUSTRALIA

Orchid bee
CENTRAL AMERICA

A Tribute to the Reptiles and Amphibians of Australia and New Zealand
Australian Herpetological Society
ISBN 978 1 92554 659 0

Australian Wildlife On Your Doorstep
Stephanie Jackson
ISBN 978 1 92554 630 9

Crocodiles of the World
Colin Stevenson
ISBN 978 1 92554 628 6

Insects of the World
Paul Zborowski
ISBN 978 1 92554 609 5

Rainforests of Australia's East Coast
Peter Krisch
ISBN 978 1 92554 629 3

Tropical Marine Life of Australia
Graham Edgar
ISBN 978 1 92151 758 7

Wild Dives
Nick and Caroline Robertson-Brown
ISBN 978 1 92554 642 2

Wild Leadership
Erna Walraven
ISBN 978 1 92554 635 4

In the same series as this title:
World of Birds
ISBN 978 1 92554 652 1

World of Reptiles
ISBN 978 1 92554 653 8

World of Mammals
ISBN 978 1 92554 660 6

For details of these books and hundreds of other Natural History titles see
www.newhollandpublishers.com
and follow ReedNewHolland
on Facebook and Instagram

First published in 2020 by Reed New Holland Publishers
Sydney • Auckland

Level 1, 178 Fox Valley Road, Wahroonga, NSW 2076, Australia
5/39 Woodside Avenue, Northcote, Auckland 0627, New Zealand

www.newhollandpublishers.com

A record of this book is held at the National Library of Australia.

ISBN 978 1 92554 651 4

Group Managing Director: Fiona Schultz
Publisher and Project Editor: Simon Papps
Designer: Andrew Davies
Production Director: Arlene Gippert
Printer: Toppan Leefung Printing Limited

10 9 8 7 6 5 4 3 2 1

Keep up with Reed New Holland
and New Holland Publishers
 ReedNewHolland
 @NewHollandPublishers and @ReedNewHolland

Front cover: Damselfly (Odonata).
Back cover: Ant (Hymenoptera).
Page 1: Moth (Lepidoptera).
Pages 2–3: Butterfly wing scales (Lepidoptera).
Pages 4–5: Fly eye (Diptera).
Page 6: Mantis (Mantodea).